OUT OF THIS WORLD
Star-Studded Haiku

For Elodie, the newest star in my family
SMW

For Lydia and June
MT

First edition 2022

Library of Congress Catalog Card Number pending
ISBN 978-1-5362-0356-1

22 23 24 25 26 APS 10 9 8 7 6 5 4 3 2 1

Printed in Humen, Dongguan, China

This book was typeset in Intro Book and Dante Regular.
The illustrations were done in mixed media.

Candlewick Press
99 Dover Street
Somerville, Massachusetts 02144

www.candlewick.com

OUT OF THIS WORLD
Star-Studded Haiku

SALLY M. WALKER

illustrated by MATTHEW TRUEMAN

CANDLEWICK PRESS

three stars in a row
Orion fastens his belt
ready for the hunt

sleuth Galileo
ponders telescopic clues
the moon's face unmasked

Hubble telescope
high above Earth's atmosphere
photographs deep space

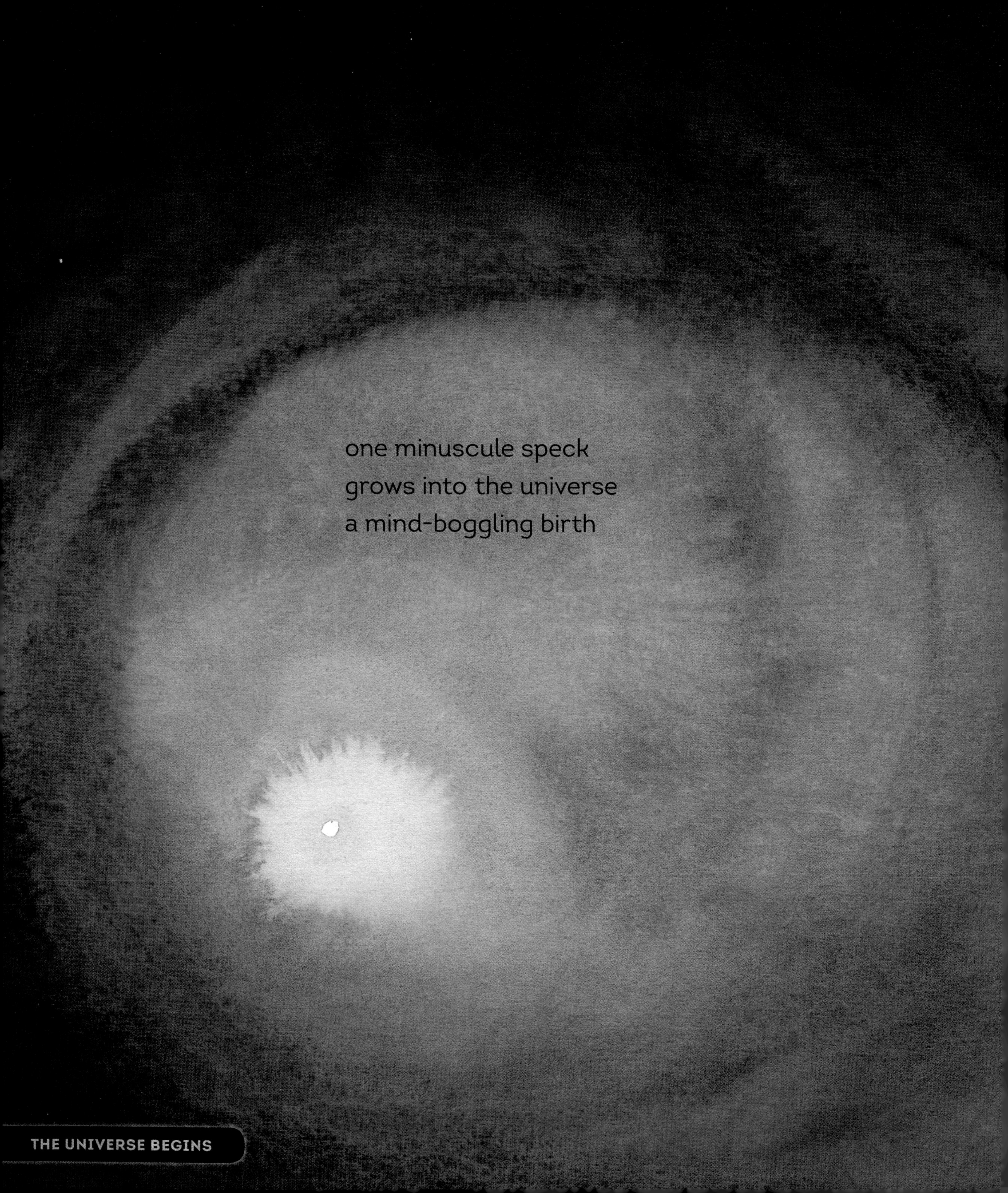

one minuscule speck
grows into the universe
a mind-boggling birth

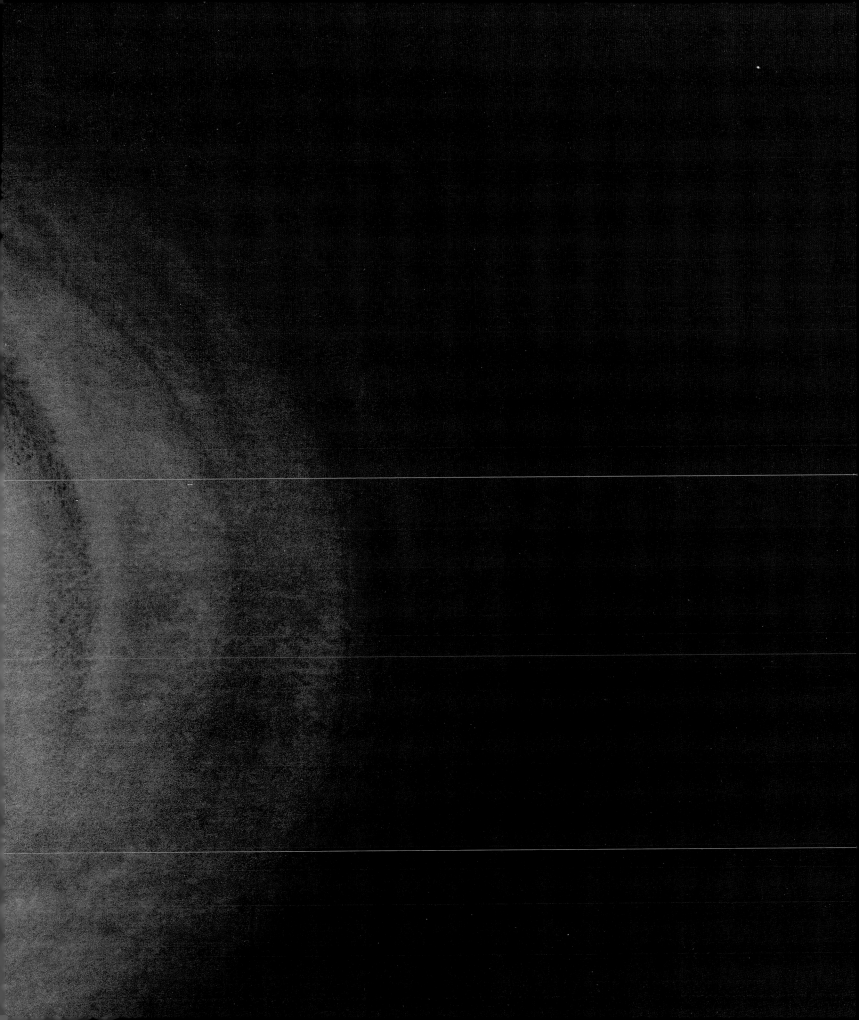

far-flung galaxies
two trillion and maybe more
resplendent cosmos

gaudy Milky Way
spiral arms blossom outward
galactic pinwheel

brilliant nebula

cloud pregnant with gas and dust

stellar nursery

distant candles flare
light glimmers through time and space
past becomes present

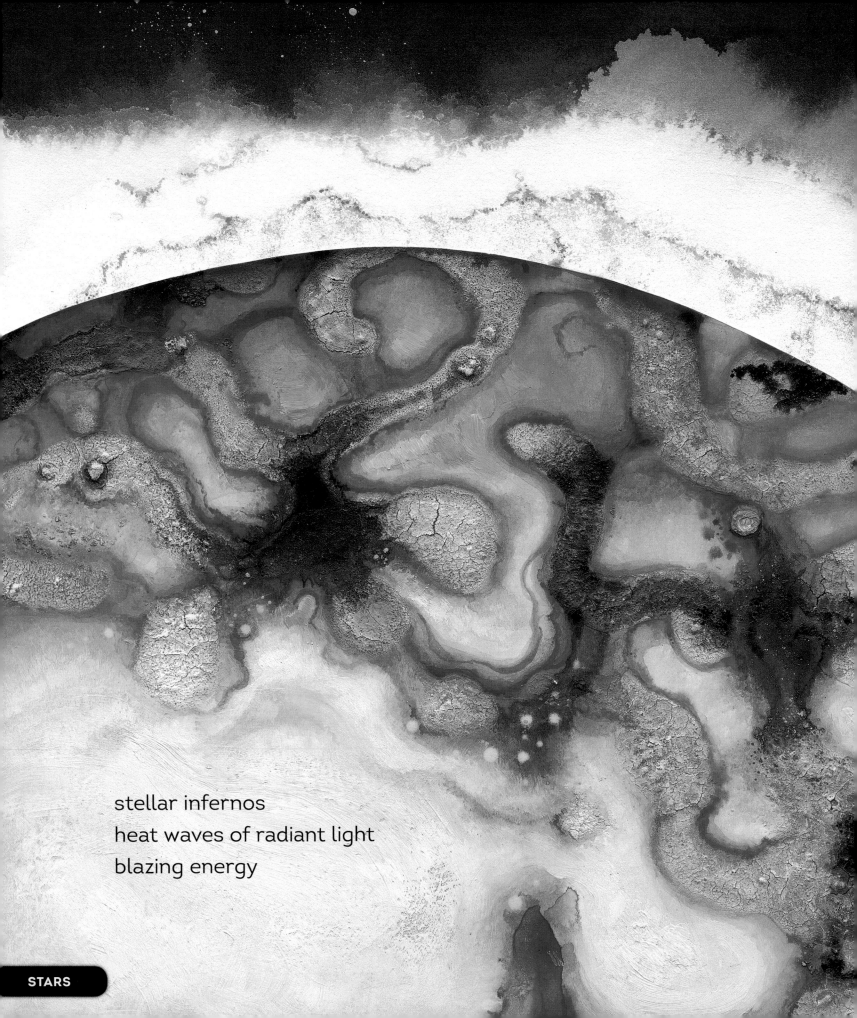

stellar infernos
heat waves of radiant light
blazing energy

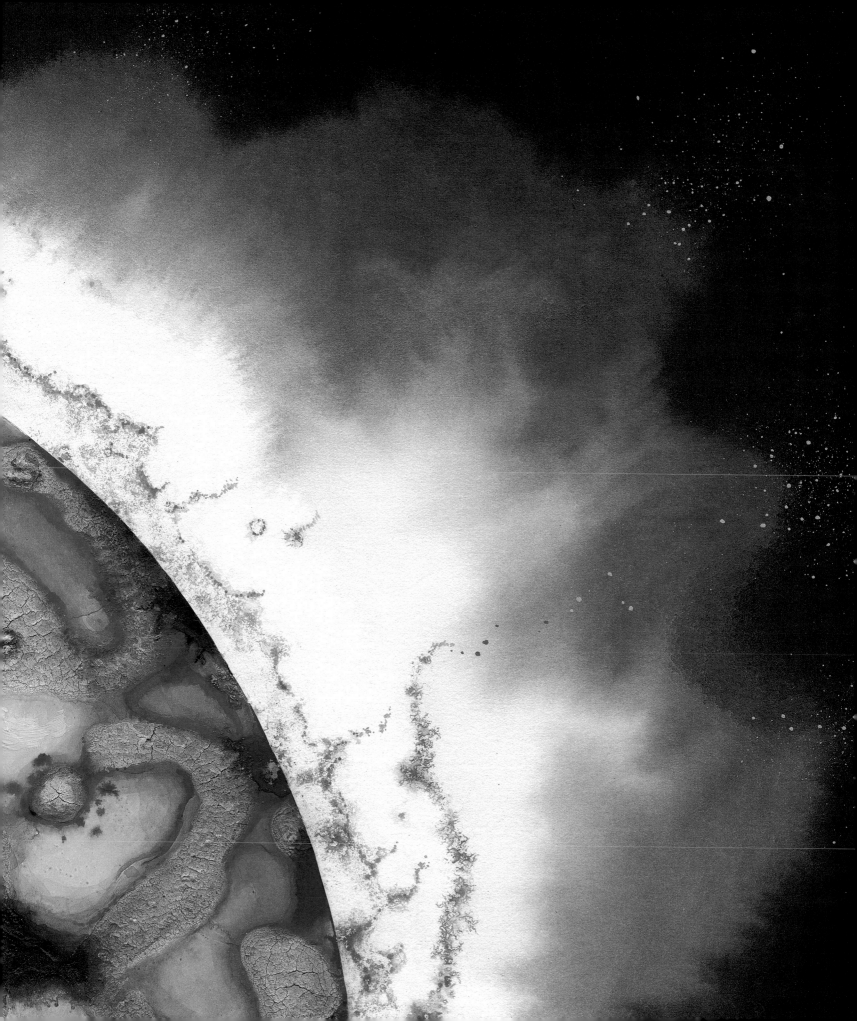

hot silver sparkles
flaming stars by the billions
fill our galaxy

hugged by gravity
eight planets bask in sunlight
solar family

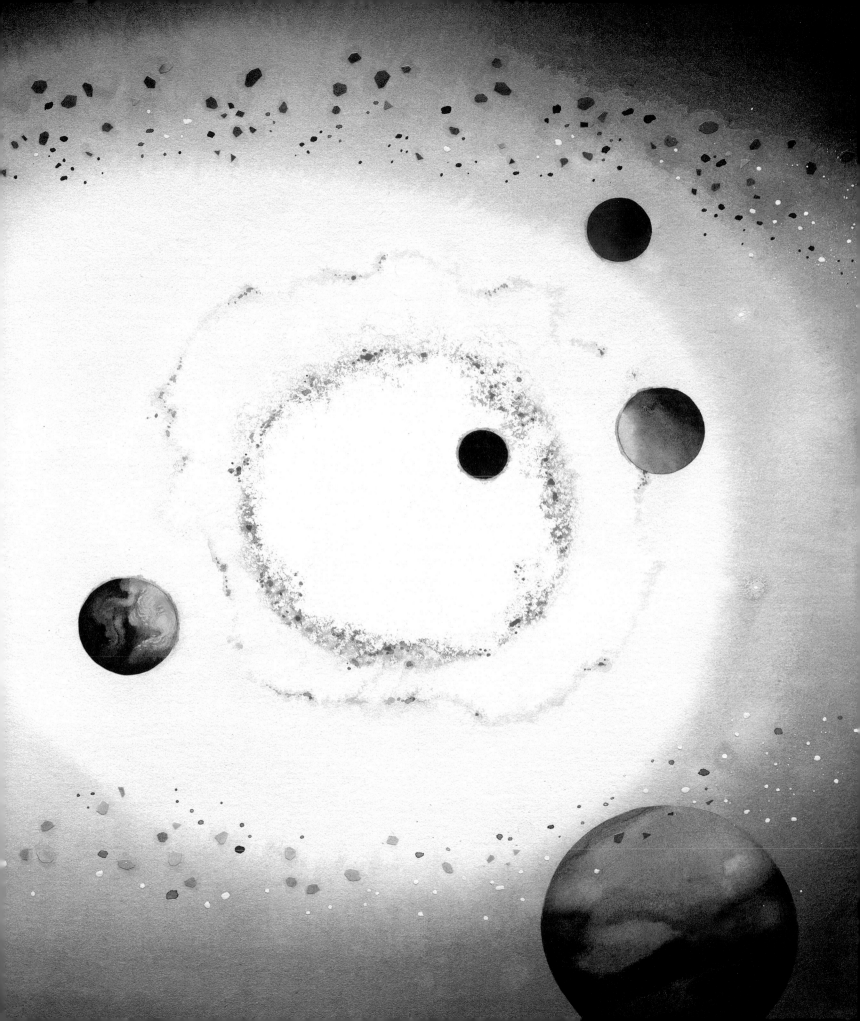

the sun's gravity
overcomes weak satellites
moonless Mercury

the smallest planet
speeds along its inside track
closest to the sun

Morning star Venus
rises before the sun wakes
and welcomes the dawn

Evening star Venus
lingers long after sunset
not ready for bed

primordial stew:
rock, atmosphere, water, life
splendiferous world

solid, liquid, gas . . .
water, water everywhere
a unique planet

cold, barren mountain
Olympus Mons volcano
an extinct dragon

Curiosity
and *Perseverance* search for
ancient life on Mars

Jupiter's red eye
stares at the solar system
a cyclops sentry

rings of rock and dust
circle around Saturn's waist
cosmic Hula-Hoops

diamonds rain, unseen,
in a slushy plasma sea
sunken treasure trove

glacier-blue Neptune
roaring winds, faster than sound,
outpace their frigid song

now a dwarf planet
Pluto still circles the sun
its heart unbroken

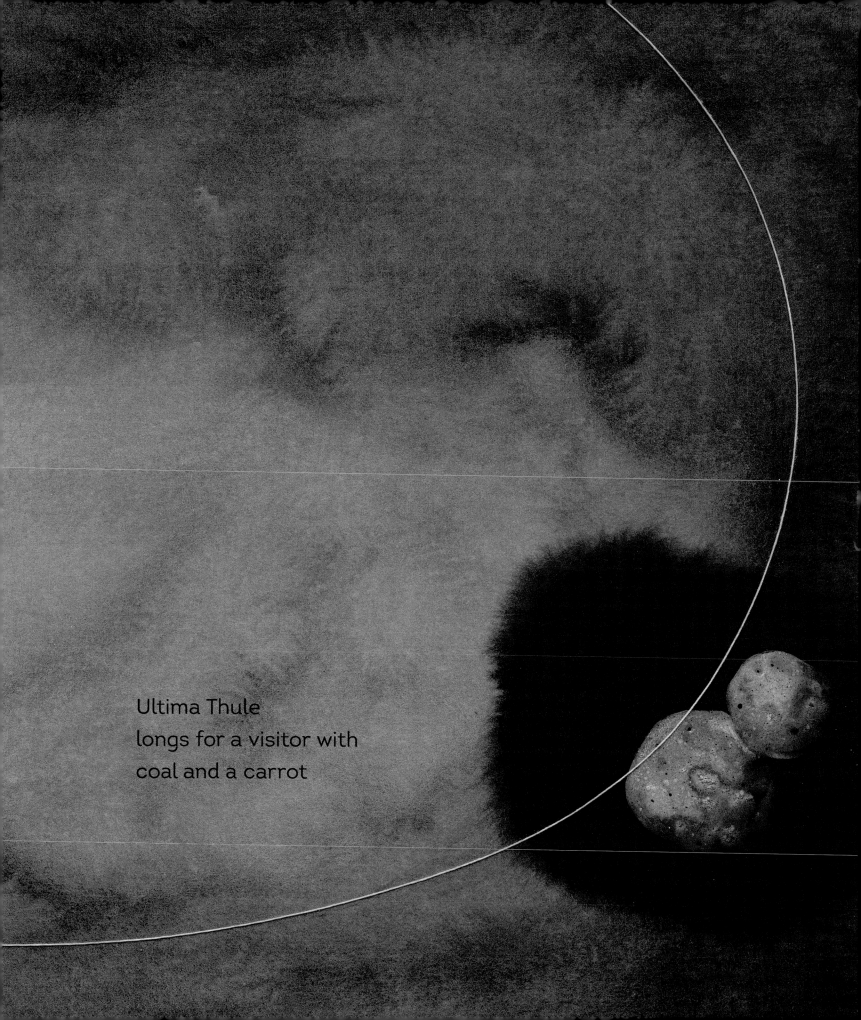

Ultima Thule
longs for a visitor with
coal and a carrot

from lunar orbit
astronauts behold earthrise
awestruck with wonder

the *Eagle* landed
"one giant leap for mankind"
footprints in the dust

playing hide-and-seek
the moon waits in Earth's shadow:
"Try to find me, Sun"

with tiny nibbles
the moon gobbles down the sun . . .
an eerie twilight

large space traveler
hits with meteoric speed
dinosaur killer

when comets swing near
the sun breathes a solar sigh
incandescent tails

shooting-star showers
sizzling streaks tumble to Earth
grains of space touch down

FURTHER EXPLORATIONS

CONSTELLATIONS AND ASTRONOMERS

People have recorded their observations of constellations—large, easily recognized star patterns—for more than 30,000 years: on bones and cave walls; on stones, clay, and paper; and, today, with computers. Ancient people connected the "star dots" to form sky pictures that represented real and mythological figures from their cultures. For example, a Greek tale describes three distinctively aligned stars as the belt that belonged to Orion the hunter. Other cultures have their own stories about the same three stars. In South Africa, they are called the Three Kings. The International Astronomical Union officially recognizes eighty-eight constellations in Earth's sky.

Astronomers discovered more about the night sky after telescopes were invented in the early 1600s. Galileo Galilei realized that the facial features of the "Man in the Moon" were actually craters. Modern super-powerful telescopes, both on Earth and on the National Aeronautics and Space Administration's

Hubble telescope in space, collect information about distant stars and galaxies with a variety of scientific techniques.

Scientists probe our solar system with remotely operated spacecraft outfitted with an array of computers and other instruments. As a space probe orbits or flies past a planet, it sends information about the planet back to Earth. Most probes send digital images that are created with data provided by computer analyses. But probes that landed on Mars sent back actual photographs of the planet's surface.

THE UNIVERSE BEGINS

Have you ever wished upon a star? On a clear night, we can see about 3,000 stars. They are part of our universe, which began as a tinier-than-minuscule point—one that was trillions of degrees hot. About fourteen billion years ago, the point changed. It rapidly expanded, creating some space as it did. Energy, or power, in the form of light instantly flooded the newly created, still infinitesimal space. Scientists call this event the Big Bang. The universe has been expanding ever since.

Within a millionth of a second after the Big Bang, changes happened. The temperature cooled a tiny bit. Subatomic particles blinked in and out of existence. They flickered back and forth between pure energy and matter. They zipped around in the rapidly growing universal brew. After about two minutes, just before the expanding universe sent them soaring apart, some particles combined. They formed the elements hydrogen, helium, and lithium, crucial ingredients for making a star. But it wasn't until about 400,000 million years *after* the Big Bang occurred that stars began to form.

After *another* 200 million years had passed, in separate areas throughout the universe, gravity began holding together large groups of stars, gas, and dust. These large groups are called galaxies. A galaxy's shape can be irregular, elliptical, or even spiral. Scientists believe the universe contains more than two *trillion* galaxies.

Earth is in the spiral-shaped Milky Way galaxy. On a clear night, stars in our galaxy may be seen as a faint band of white light across the sky. Ancient Chinese astronomers thought it looked like a silver river. Greek astronomers thought it looked like a milky circle of light, hence the name Milky Way. (No cow was involved!) It wasn't until 1610, after telescopes had been invented, that Italian astronomer Galileo Galilei examined the band with a telescope and saw that it was actually the combined light of countless individual stars. Astronomers estimate that the Milky Way contains at least 100 billion stars. Larger galaxies likely contain trillions of stars.

STARS

A nebula is a cloud of gas and dust found in space. When a nebula collapses, its center gets hot and dense.

Gravity holds the material together. If more gas and dust are added, a star may form. You can wish upon a star, but you can't stand on one. Stars don't have solid land; they're made of superheated gases. A star's extremely high temperature causes gas atoms to break apart. When they do, they form a state of matter called plasma. The atomic particles that form plasma have lots of energy. Some of the energy produces flashes of light, which is what we see.

Space is so vast that writing the distances in regular measurements, such as miles or kilometers, would take too much room. Instead, astronomers measure space distances in light-years. One light-year equals the distance that light can travel in one Earth year (365 days). In a vacuum, like space, light travels at 186,000 miles (299,000 kilometers) *per second*. At that speed, one light-year equals 5.9 trillion miles (9.5 trillion kilometers).

The sun is a star. Even though it dwarfs the planets in our solar system, it isn't the universe's biggest star. A star named UY Scuti, located 9,500 light-years from Earth, currently holds that honor. This whale of a star has a radius that is 1,700 times longer than the sun's!

A flash of light emitted by the sun takes a little longer than eight minutes to reach Earth. Each ray of sunlight we see is actually how the sun looked eight minutes ago. The next closest stars to Earth are a system of three stars called Alpha Centauri. They are slightly more than four light-years away from Earth, about 25 trillion miles (40 trillion kilometers). The light we see from Alpha Centauri is more than four years old by the time we see it. When we look at a distant star, we see how it looked some time ago. A star's past is our present. The farther away in space that a telescope or spacecraft explores, the farther back into space-time we are able to see.

OUR SOLAR SYSTEM

The **SUN** is the star closest to Earth. When a star is the center of a solar system, it is called a sun. It's endless summer in the sun's core, where the temperature is about 27 million°F (15 million°C).

Eight planets orbit the sun, held in place by the sun's gravity. How long it takes each planet to orbit the sun varies. It takes Earth about 365 days, the time period that we call a year. As a planet orbits the sun, it also rotates, or spins, on its axis. It takes Earth twenty-four hours to complete one rotation. We call this one day.

A planet's gravity rounds it into a sphere. The four planets closest to the sun—Mercury, Venus, Earth, and Mars—are made of rock and metals. Scientists call them the terrestrial planets, from the Latin word that means "land" or "ground."

MERCURY

Average distance from the sun 36 million miles (58 million km)
Diameter 3,032 miles (4,880 km)
Orbit around the sun 88 Earth days
Revolution (one day-and-night cycle) 176 Earth days

Mercury, the smallest planet, is the closest to the sun. The sun's radiation on Mercury is so strong that the *Messenger* spacecraft, launched by NASA in 2004, wore a special shield to protect it while it orbited the planet from 2011 to 2015.

VENUS

Average distance from the sun 67 million miles (108 million km)
Diameter 7,521 miles (12,104 km)
Orbit around the sun 225 Earth days
Revolution (one day-and-night cycle) 243 Earth days

Venus is similar in size to Earth, but is much hotter. The average temperature is 867°F (464°C). Of the eight planets in our solar system, only Venus rotates around its axis from east to west (counterclockwise). So on Venus, the sun rises in the west! Also, each Venutian *day* lasts longer than a Venutian *year*.

Venus is often called the Morning Star or the Evening Star. (But remember, it's a planet, not a star!) Which one depends on the planet's position along its solar orbit. At times, a viewer from Earth can see Venus before sunrise in the eastern sky. Months later, after Venus has traveled farther along its orbital path and overtaken, or passed, Earth, it appears after sunset in the western sky. After the sun and the moon, Venus and Jupiter are the two brightest objects in Earth's sky.

EARTH

Average distance from the sun 93 million miles (150 million km)
Diameter 7,918 miles (12,743 km)
Orbit around the sun 365 days (one year)
Revolution (one day-and-night cycle) 24 hours

Earth, sometimes called the Blue Planet, has a surface that is unique in our solar system: it has water, the liquid made from atoms of hydrogen and oxygen. On other planets, water has not been found as liquid. It is only found as ice and vapor. Oceans cover about 70 percent of Earth's surface and give the planet its blue color. Earth's distance from the sun perfectly situated it for life—as we know it—to flourish.

MARS

Average distance from the sun 142 million miles (228 million km)
Diameter 4,212 miles (6,780 km)
Orbit around the sun 687 Earth days
Revolution (one day-and-night cycle) 24 hours, 42 minutes

Mars, the terrestrial planet farthest from the sun, is scarred with deep channels and swirly patterns.

Because moving water causes these kinds of land features on Earth, scientists believe that water once flowed on Mars. Now water exists on Mars only as ice caps at its north and south poles and as vapor in the atmosphere. Mars is often called the Red Planet. Its dusty soil contains a lot of the element iron. When iron chemically reacts with oxygen, it forms reddish-brown rust, giving Mars its red color. Olympus Mons, the largest volcano in our solar system, is on Mars.

The NASA spacecraft *Curiosity* landed on Mars in 2012. In 2018, *Curiosity* collected rock samples. Analyses of the samples contained some of the chemical building blocks that are necessary for some forms of life that live on Earth. Scientists plan to use *Perseverance*'s seven-foot-long jointed robotic arm to drill into the surface and collect more rock samples. Information gathered by *Curiosity* and *Perseverance* may someday answer the question *Did life once exist on Mars?*

The four planets farthest from the sun—Jupiter, Saturn, Uranus, and Neptune—are called the gas giants. They do not have a solid land surface.

JUPITER

Average distance from the sun 484 million miles (779 million km)
Diameter 88,846 miles (142,984 km)
Orbit around the sun 11.8 Earth years
Revolution (one day-and-night cycle) 9 hours, 54 minutes

Jupiter, the closest of the gas giants, is definitely gigantic: more than 1,300 Earths could be packed inside it! Jupiter's Great Red Spot is a huge storm, bigger than the Earth is wide, that's been raging for at least 150 years. Gusty winds peak at about 400 miles (644 kilometers) per hour.

SATURN

Average distance from the sun 891 million miles (1.4 billion km)
Diameter 74,897 miles (120,536 km)
Orbit around the sun 29 Earth years
Revolution (one day-and-night cycle) 10 hours, 40 minutes

Saturn is the second largest planet in the solar system. When Galileo saw Saturn's rings, he had no idea what they were. Telescopes and spacecraft invented in later centuries revealed the rings' secret: they are particles of ice or rock covered with ice. Scientists theorize that the rings that surround this gassy giant may be the remains of a moon that broke apart.

Because Saturn is made mostly of gas, it could float in water. But finding an ocean large enough to hold it isn't possible—at least in our solar system!

URANUS

Average distance from the sun 1.8 billion miles (2.9 billion km)
Diameter 31,763 miles (51,118 km)
Orbit around the sun 84 Earth years
Revolution (one day-and-night cycle) 17 hours, 14 minutes

Uranus, the third gas giant, stands alone—or perhaps, *lies* alone—in a unique way. An axis is a straight line around which a planet rotates. The axes of all the planets in our solar system run through the planets' north and south poles. Seven of these axes are somewhat tilted, so their planets' equators face the sun. But Uranus's axis is tipped sideways, as if it were lying down. This means that Uranus's north and south poles, not its equator, alternately face the sun. Scientists theorize that a series of collisions knocked the planet into its current position.

Another oddity occurs inside the planet. A slushy plasma ocean surrounds Uranus's solid core. It contains lots of carbon—the element that forms diamonds. Extremely high pressure within the ocean forces carbon atoms to crystallize into diamonds. Heavier than the surrounding slush, the diamonds rain toward the planet's core.

NEPTUNE

Average distance from the sun 2.8 billion miles (4.5 billion km)
Diameter 30,775 miles (49,528 km)
Orbit around the sun 165 Earth years
Revolution (one day-and-night cycle) 16 hours

Neptune, the farthest planet from the sun, has the highest winds in the solar system, clocked at 1,500 miles (2,400 kilometers) per hour, three times faster than the winds of Jupiter's Great Red Spot. Methane gas high in Neptune's atmosphere gives Neptune its blue color. Methane absorbs red light waves that come from the sun. It reflects the sun's blue light waves back into space. Those blue waves are what our eyes see, but only with the help of a powerful telescope. Neptune is so far away that it isn't visible otherwise.

PLUTO, a celestial body beyond Neptune, was discovered in 1930. It was considered the ninth planet until 2006, when the International Astronomical Union reclassified it as a dwarf planet. Photos of Pluto show a large heart-shaped feature on its surface. Massive amounts of ice form the bright, smooth feature.

ULTIMA THULE is a space body four billion miles (6.4 billion kilometers) from the sun. In the images sent by the spacecraft *New Horizons*, it looks like a snowman. Ultima Thule (TOO-lee) is deep in a donut-shaped area of space called the Kuiper Belt. Scientists think that it formed when two separate balls of ice collided, each one moving at a speed slow enough that neither one broke when they bumped. The smaller of the two icy balls is about 9 miles (15 kilometers) across; the larger about 12 miles (19 kilometers). Ultima Thule is made of materials that are 4.5 billion years old. So, it's possible that this intriguing space snowman may hold the secrets of our solar system's origin.

MOONS AND ECLIPSES

A moon is a celestial body that orbits a planet. Although there are many moons in our solar system, neither Mercury nor Venus has one. The sun's strong gravity pulls would-be moons away from Mercury and absorbs them. Venus's moonless sky is a yet unsolved mystery. Earth has one moon. The remaining five planets in our solar system have multiple moons, most of which can be seen only with telescopes or by spacecraft. Saturn has at least fifty-three moons; Jupiter may have as many as seventy-nine!

Many moons are made of rock and ice. So far, scientists haven't discovered any with surface water. But they believe some may have hidden water, even oceans, buried beneath their icy surface. Some moons, such as Io, one of Jupiter's moons, have active volcanoes.

Earth's moon formed about 4.5 billion years ago when a Mars-size object slammed into Earth. Rock debris from Earth's mantle (one of the planet's inner layers) flew into space. The debris circled our planet, held in orbit by Earth's gravity. Over time, pieces of the debris collided, combined, and became Earth's moon.

The moon used to have active volcanoes, but they have been extinct for more than three billion years. The craters that scar the moon's surface are the result of meteor impacts—old and new—not volcanoes.

Earth's moon has no atmosphere. Since there is no atmospheric movement, no water, wind, or ice changes the moon's surface. Footprints made by the astronauts who have walked on the moon still remain in the lunar dust. On July 20, 1969, when Apollo 11 astronaut Neil Armstrong stepped onto the lunar surface—the first human ever to do so—he said, "That's one small step for (a) man; one giant leap for mankind."

A lunar eclipse occurs when Earth's orbit positions it between the sun and the moon. As Earth moves into this position, its shadow creeps across the face of the moon. For a few moments during a total lunar eclipse, the moon seems to vanish.

Sometimes the moon's orbit places it between Earth and the sun. The moon slowly blocks sunlight from reaching Earth. An eerie twilight forms. During a total eclipse, the moon completely blocks our view of the sun. For a few seconds, day becomes night. The sun appears as a thin ring of bright light. Unless you are wearing special protective glasses, you should never look directly at a solar eclipse. The rays will damage your retinas and can lead to blindness.

ASTEROIDS, COMETS, AND METEORS

Asteroids, comets, and meteors are space rocks that orbit the sun. Scientific analyses of pieces that have fallen to Earth suggest they are leftover material from our solar system's birth. If so, they may be 4.6 billion years old!

Asteroids are the largest space rocks. Millions of asteroids exist between the orbits of Mars and Jupiter in an area known as the asteroid belt. Vast distances—thousands, possibly millions, of miles—separate them. Made of rock and iron, asteroids range in size from a few miles up to hundreds of miles long.

Scientists theorize that a mountain-size asteroid impacted Earth 65 million years ago. It triggered catastrophic events that killed off more than 70 percent of Earth's creatures, including large dinosaurs.

Comets are space snowballs made of frozen gases and dust. Most comets in our solar system exist in the Kuiper Belt. This belt is in the far reaches of our solar system and extends beyond Neptune's orbit, out into the area that includes the dwarf planet Pluto. The Kuiper Belt is where the earliest materials that formed our solar system are found.

We see a comet when it develops a fiery tail. As a comet nears the sun, solar heat vaporizes part of the comet's outer layer. It pushes out a trail (or tail) of hot debris. Because the vaporized material is pushed out by the sun's radiation, a comet's tail always points away from the sun. When a comet approaches the sun, its tail streams behind it. But when a comet moves away from the sun, its tail stretches out in *front* of it.

Meteors are the smallest space rocks, probably created when larger space rocks collide and shatter. Traveling at speeds up to 100,000 miles (161,000 kilometers) per hour, meteors often zoom into Earth's atmosphere. When they do, they become "shooting stars." Most meteors vaporize as they fall, but thousands of them hit the ground each year. Then they are called meteorites. Fortunately, most of them are small by the time they hit—the size of a grain of sand—so they don't cause noticeable damage.

GLOSSARY

axis a straight line through the center of an object, around which the object spins

core the center of a planet or star

cosmos the orderly, whole system of the universe

crystallize to solidify in a pattern

cyclops a one-eyed giant found in Greek and Roman mythology

eclipse an event that occurs when the shadow of one celestial body is temporarily cast onto another celestial body

glacier a massive body of slowly moving ice

gravity the force that draws one body to another

light a form of rapidly moving energy that we can see

nebula a gigantic cloud of hot gases and dust

orbit a circular or elliptical path that a celestial object follows as it moves around a larger body

plasma a gas-like collection of charged particles with lots of energy; the fourth state of matter

revolution a complete 360-degree turn

satellite an object or astronomical body, held in place by gravity, that orbits a larger astronomical body

solar orbit the path that an astronomical body, such as a planet or comet, follows when it travels around the sun

spacecraft a vehicle that is used to explore space

FURTHER READING

Couper, Heather, Robert Dinwiddie, et. al. *The Planets: The Definitive Visual Guide to Our Solar System*. New York: Dorling Kindersley, 2014.

Hamblin, W. Kenneth, and Eric H. Christiansen. *Earth's Dynamic Systems*. 10th ed. Upper Saddle River, NJ: Prentice Hall, 2004.

Liu, Charles. *The Handy Astronomy Answer Book*. Canton, MI: Visible Ink, 2014.

Prinja, Raman and Chris Wormell. *Planetarium: Welcome to the Museum*. Somerville, MA: Candlewick Press, 2019.

Ride, Sally, and Tam O'Shaughnessy. *Voyager: An Adventure to the Edge of the Solar System*. New York: Crown, 1992.

Trefil, James. *Space Atlas: Mapping the Universe and Beyond*. Washington, DC: National Geographic Society, 2012.

Wood, Matthew Brenden. *Planetary Science: Explore New Frontiers*. White River Junction, VT: Nomad, 2017.

ONLINE RESOURCES

The Archaeology News Network
https://archaeologynewsnetwork.blogspot.com/2015/07/5000-year-old-carvings-on-irish-cairn.html

NASA Goddard YouTube Channel
Listen to the Apollo 8 crew's reaction to earthrise at:
https://www.youtube.com/watch?v=LHbFIieK-uo

NASA Science Solar System Exploration
https://solarsystem.nasa.gov

NASA Science Space Place
https://spaceplace.nasa.gov

Phys.org
https://phys.org
This website features up-to-date science, research, and technology information about a variety of scientific fields, including space physics.

Windows to the Universe
https://www.windows2universe.org
This site, by the National Earth Science Teachers Association, explores many space topics with information presented at beginner, intermediate, and advanced levels.